H.E.A.L.T.H. I.S.S.U.E.S.

HODDER
Wayland

an imprint of Hodder Children's Books

White-Thomson Publishing Ltd,
2-3 St Andrew's Place, Lewes,
East Sussex BN7 1UP

Published in Great Britain in 2004 by Hodder Wayland, an imprint of Hodder Children's Books

This paperback edition published in 2005

This book was produced for White-Thomson Publishing Ltd by Ruth Nason.

Design: Carole Binding
Picture research: Glass Onion Pictures

The right of Karla Fitzhugh to be identified as the author of this work has been asserted by her in accordance with the Copyright, Designs and Patents Act 1988.

British Library Cataloguing in Publication Data
Fitzhugh, Karla
    Body Image. - (Health Issues)
    1. Body image - Juvenile literature
    I. Title
    306.4

ISBN 0 7502 4482 8

Printed by C&C Offset Printing Co., Ltd. China

Hodder Children's Books
A division of Hodder Headline Limited
338 Euston Road, London NW1 3BH

Acknowledgements
The author and publishers thank the following for their permission to reproduce photographs and illustrations: Corbis: pages 6b (George Disario), 9 (Francis G. Mayer), 11 (Jon Feingersh), 15 (Gabe Palmer), 16 (Steve Prezant), 32 (Hekimian Julien/Corbis Sygma), 33 (Larry Williams), 44 (Paul Edmondson), 51 (LWA-Dann Tardif), 59 (Jose Luis Pelaez, Inc.); Popperfoto.com: page 21; Rex Features: pages 13, 20, 29, 34, 37, 46, 48; Science Photo Library: pages 4 (Oscar Burriel), 18 (Mauro Fermariello), 24 (Alain Dex, Publiphoto Diffusion), 27 (Oscar Burriel), 39 (BSIP Barrelle), 49 (Alex Bartel), 53 (Hank Morgan); Topham/ImageWorks: cover and pages 1, 22, 30, 40, 55, 56; Topham/Photri: page 6t.

Note: Photographs illustrating the case studies in this book were posed by models.

Every effort has been made to trace copyright holders. However, the publishers apologise for any unintentional omissions and would be pleased in such cases to add an acknowledgement in any future editions.

158.1

Contents

Introduction
All in the mind?

Body image is 'subjective': in other words, it's to do with the way we think and feel about ourselves and others, rather than exact measurements or facts. It can strongly affect how good or bad we feel about ourselves and our lives. Many people feel deeply dissatisfied with the way that they look, even though they are fit and healthy, and this can lead to general unhappiness or unhealthy behaviours. Being comfortable in your own body, however it looks or moves, makes it much easier to like yourself and take care of yourself physically and emotionally.

What is body image?

Many factors add up to make someone's body image. It is more than just physical appearance, attractiveness, or beauty. It can be very complex, and includes physical sensations from the body, your emotions, and your thoughts. Body image is a product of our minds and our imaginations, rather than a 'fact' or something that is fixed or set in stone. A person's body image can change from day to day, or over longer periods of time.

The main factors of body image are:

⊚ the physical sensations in our bodies and our awareness of them;

⊚ how we picture ourselves in our minds, including our size and shape;

⊚ how we think others see us and judge us;

⊚ our beliefs, judgements and feelings about our bodies.

So, it appears that body image is mostly psychological, or 'all in the mind'. It has more to do with self-esteem and

Mind over mirror
The reflection you see when you look at yourself in a mirror is affected by the way you picture yourself in your mind.

how much we like and value ourselves generally than it has to do with how other people may look at us.

People are not born with a particular body image. It is something they learn as they grow up. Much of what we learn comes from family and friends, and this usually reflects the type of society that we live in. The media also has a strong influence, so we may pick up on subtle messages from television shows, advertisements, cinema, magazines, books and the internet. Teenagers in particular are affected very strongly by body image, partly because their bodies are growing and changing shape, and partly because they often feel lots of pressure to 'fit in' with friends and be well-liked and popular. They often end up thinking, wrongly, that the best way to be popular or accepted is by looking a specific way, or by having 'the perfect body'.

People often try to change their appearance and body image to try to look or feel a certain way, usually to try to fit in with what they think society expects of them. This includes wearing particular clothes, grooming themselves (washing regularly, using make-up or other cosmetic products, having a particular hairstyle and so on), eating particular foods, exercising and visiting the dentist. Others may go much further with changes and perhaps lose lots of weight, take drugs such as anabolic steroids, or undergo surgery to alter the way they look.

'I often find myself thinking that if I looked a bit more glamorous, maybe life would be much easier for me. Perhaps people would treat me better.'
(Kelly, aged 13)

Positive body image

Body image is linked with health in several ways. When people have a positive body image, they tend to feel good about themselves generally and in touch with their bodies, and this can lead to them looking after themselves in a healthy way. This may mean having a balanced diet, taking time out to relax or pamper themselves, avoiding drug abuse, and keeping fit. They tend to groom themselves well, but not obsessively, and wear clothes and hairstyles that suit and flatter their natural features. They develop confidence in their physical abilities, feel comfortable with who they are and find it easy to care for themselves.

Negative body image

When people have a poor body image, they can end up feeling unhappy or even downright depressed about themselves as people. They may also be tempted to make drastic alterations to their lifestyles or bodies that can affect their health in a negative way. Negative body image ranges from mild through to extreme feelings and thoughts, and can give rise to all kinds of different behaviours. Most people have the occasional 'bad hair day', when they feel mildly annoyed or unhappy with the way they look for a short time, but they then start to feel better in a day or two. Extreme obsessions with body image can bring on strong feelings of unhappiness and unattractiveness, which can be so bad that they make living a normal life almost impossible.

Many things are thought to contribute to someone developing a negative body image, such as:

- not being cuddled or touched much as a baby, and feeling out of touch with their own body;
- being teased about appearance as a child or teenager;
- growing up with parents who are dieting, have eating disorders, or speak about disliking their own bodies;

Teenagers
Teenagers may become very sensitive about their appearance, as their bodies change during puberty. For example, having acne can be distressing.

Orthodontics
Treatment to straighten teeth (orthodontics) is the most common cosmetic procedure for teenagers.

- being neglected and abused during childhood;
- looking different from classmates, for example having skin or growth problems;
- being around people who judge others only by the way they look;
- peer pressure to be thin, muscular, on a diet, or dressed in a particular way;
- promotion of fad diets in the media;
- use of very thin or muscular models in fashion magazines and advertisements;
- public health programmes aimed at preventing obesity, which may backfire when people mistakenly think they are overweight.

People with a negative body image often wrongly think that their appearance is the most important thing about themselves, and is the key to success in life. Even if they are a healthy weight, they may pick on themselves for being 'too fat' or the 'wrong shape'. They may also think that there is only one 'right' way to look, or yearn to be 'perfect'. The more desperate they become to look a particular way, the more likely they are to try anything to get a quick fix, or look for a short cut. Looks become more important to them than health, or feeling comfortable. They are more likely to starve themselves than make slower, more long-term changes such as eating a balanced diet and taking a little regular exercise. They may also exercise themselves to the point of exhaustion or injury, or be tempted to take drugs to change their appearance. Controlling their looks becomes a full-time preoccupation and can take over their lives completely. Even if they do end up looking how they wish to, they may still not be happy.

'If I'm feeling down about something, I've noticed I start being negative about my face and body too. I've learned to ignore it because when I cheer up again, I'm not so down about the way I look.' (Adam, aged 15)

Low self-esteem and body image

People who feel bad about themselves overall often find that their low self-esteem affects their body image. For example, they may feel that it isn't worth looking after themselves or trying to live a healthy life, so they may neglect their personal hygiene and clothing, not eat healthily or take enough exercise, or not see a doctor if they have health problems.

Sometimes a person who has low self-esteem may behave as though they are punishing themselves. There are many reasons why people might deliberately harm themselves, but self-hatred or self-loathing may make some people cut or burn their skin, starve themselves, or pull out their own hair, which has further negative effects on their body image.

About this book

This book looks at both the positive and negative sides of body image. Chapter 1 is about the messages we get from society about our appearances. It looks at how particular appearances have gone in and out of fashion over time, and how what's considered 'attractive' can vary from culture to culture. Chapter 2 covers issues such as body size, shape, fitness and healthy eating. It also investigates problems such as fad diets, anorexia nervosa, bulimia, compulsive eating and steroid abuse. 'Skin-deep' concerns are looked at in Chapter 3, where issues such as grooming, piercing tattooing and tanning are covered. Skin problems such as acne, eczema and psoriasis are included in this chapter too.

In Chapter 4 we look at the changes that happen during growth and puberty, both physical and emotional. Chapter 5 is about cosmetic and plastic surgery, concentrating on the operations that are most commonly performed, and the health and safety issues that surround them. Finally, in Chapter 6, several ways to improve body image are explored, to attempt to change thought and behaviour patterns in a positive way to help ourselves and others. The Glossary on page 62 explains any unfamiliar words or phrases that have been used, and the Resources section suggests some useful sources of futher information and specialist support.

Help

It's entirely normal to feel down about your appearance sometimes. The list of 'signs' on page 54 will help you decide whether you do have a problem with your body image.

1 Changing ideals
The rise of physical culture

Body image is strongly influenced by family, friends and society. We also receive subtle or not-so-subtle messages about what type of appearance is 'ideal' or 'desirable' from television, films and magazines. Human beings have a tendency to read too much into a person's appearance, so it's not surprising that many of us think we will get special treatment if we look a certain way.

Appearances throughout history

What people think of as beautiful, handsome or healthy has changed dramatically over the centuries. A person from nineteenth-century Europe, or an American Pioneer, would probably look at one of today's heart-throb actors or top models and wonder what all the fuss was about, because times are so different.

What's been considered 'attractive' has often mirrored signs of wealth or high social status, or what was thought to be 'good health'. For a long time, having a high proportion of body fat was fashionable, because it meant that you were from a background where you had more than enough to eat and were probably rich. It also suggested that you were free from diseases that would make you look strained or physically wasted, such as tuberculosis. Historically, pale skin was seen as attractive in many cultures because it

Past ideals
Paintings like those of Rubens (1577-1640) show ideals of beauty from the past.

meant that you were rich and could afford to stay indoors and avoid hard physical labour. Painters such as Rubens recorded images of the great beauties of the age. Rich men wore fine clothes and enhanced their appearance with wigs and cosmetics.

In eighteenth-century America, both female and male Pioneers were considered attractive if they were large, muscular, tough and strong. It may have been an advantage in surviving hardships, and in working the land as farmers. By the nineteenth century, the fashionable appearance for women in Europe and America had changed radically, compared to men. Women were expected to be fragile, thin and pale. A small waist was thought attractive, and most women wore corsets to force themselves into this shape. Corsets sometimes broke women's ribs, squashed the internal organs and made it difficult to move around and eat and breathe freely.

'I'm quite well rounded, and the other day a make-up lady said to me that if I'd lived in the sixteenth century, I would have been one of the most beautiful women alive. I thought great, that's not much use to me now!' (Liora, actress)

Corsets went out of fashion in the 1920s, as women became more of a force in the workplace, and more sporty. In Europe during the Second World War in the 1940s, women took up work in factories or did heavy farm work, and the ideal changed again to strong, capable and muscular. Things were different once more in the 1950s, as ordinary women tried to look like Hollywood glamour girls. Most of these actresses looked curvy, including Marilyn Monroe. Many of them secretly had cosmetic surgery. Sun tans were popular, perhaps because they were a sign that someone was rich and could afford holidays in the sun. Men that were thought of as handsome often had very 'masculine' faces with square jaws and cleft or dimpled chins. 'Manly' actors included John Wayne and Burt Lancaster.

Body fat

Curvy actress Marilyn Monroe looks large compared to today's actresses, but she was a healthy weight for her height, and had around 20% body fat, which is fairly slim. On average, the big movie actresses of today have less body fat than the popular actresses of the 1950s.

By the 1960s and '70s, models such as Twiggy were much thinner than before, and had boyish figures. During this time the health food movement started to take off, but most people considered it strange or cranky. From the 1980s onwards, highly muscular male bodies with very low body fat were seen in films and used more commonly in advertisements. Many male models now had slightly more 'feminine' facial features such as large eyes and lips. Tall, athletic-looking female models such as Elle McPherson, Cindy Crawford and Naomi Campbell came into fashion. Ordinary people began to take much more of an interest in what they ate, and joined gyms or attended aerobics classes in greater numbers. Shortly after this, the 'waif' look became popular again, and very thin girls like Kate Moss were in the limelight.

Body image and the media

People who are considered 'attractive' and are put on display by the media usually fall into a very narrow range of appearances. They tend to be

Present ideals

Since the 1980s, a healthy, toned appearance has been what many people aim for and consider attractive.

Around the world

What the West calls beautiful may be considered unattractive in other societies. We may be obsessed about slimness, but in more traditional societies such as the Pacific Islands of Tonga and Western Samoa, having a large proportion of body fat is associated with a nurturing or royal image. It is still popular with many older men and women on the islands, in spite of the health problems it can cause.

My best friends

'I think people just look at the surface too much, and assume things. Look at my best friends. One of them is kind of big-boned, but not overweight. He gets up early most mornings and takes the family dog out for a run, and plays tennis twice a week. He eats right, and doesn't smoke or take drugs. The other friend never does any exercise, skips breakfast, and is fairly thin. He lives on soft drinks and chips, smokes, and lies in the sun for hours without sunscreen. He doesn't respect his body at all, but people take one look at both my friends and they instantly assume that the thinner one is the healthiest one. The story just isn't that simple. Maybe it will show up more when we're older."
(Nathan, aged 15)

tall, young, smooth-skinned, very slim and toned, and their faces are usually symmetrical and have large eyes and wide mouths. Women who are held up in this way are often white, blonde, blue-eyed and tanned. The vast majority of people do not fall into this group; in fact, over 99% of the population do not live up to the 'ideal'. That certainly does not mean that they are unattractive. People of all shapes, sizes and races can be attractive.

In the last few years, people have become more and more obsessed with the lives of celebrities such as TV stars, athletes, actors, pop stars and models. There are more magazines, gossip columns and television shows devoted to them than ever before, and many ordinary people try to imitate their looks and lifestyles. Hairstyles, cosmetics, jewellery and clothes are often copied, especially by teenagers who want to look like their favourite stars. What many people don't realize is that looking good is a full-time job for most celebrities.

Someone who relies on their looks for a living often spends many hours each day at the gym, perhaps with a personal trainer. They may be on a permanent diet, or take drugs to keep their weight down or increase their muscles, even if they say they do no such thing. Cosmetic surgery and other cosmetic procedures are commonly relied upon, and even then celebrities still have days when they don't look their best. Flattering lighting, huge amounts of make-up, skilled camera work, top stylists and special effects are needed to create that 'perfect' appearance. Even then, images may be air-brushed or digitally altered to get the right look.

Advertisements and music videos exist to sell things, not to make the viewer feel good, although they can be very clever and entertaining. They often use digitally altered images of models to grab attention. Sometimes they are designed to make you feel insecure, or worry about your attractiveness or the way other people might see you. It's a way of making you think that your life would be better if you bought their product. Some adverts for cosmetics, diet products and fitness equipment can be misleading or completely dishonest.

Camera chase

Celebrities are pursued by photographers trying to catch the 'best' photographs, which will be published in celebrity magazines. Why do you think these are popular?

Body image and the individual

Men, women and children are becoming more and more dissatisfied with their appearances. In an American study by *Psychology Today* in 1997, 56% of adult women and 43% of men said they were dissatisfied with their appearance in general. The number of men who don't like their appearance has almost trebled in the last twenty years, and the number of women who say the same thing has doubled. The women were most likely to complain about their stomachs, body weight and hips. The men were most likely to complain about being underweight or not muscular enough. Other studies suggest that up to 80% of women do not like the way they look.

There has also been a sharp increase in the number of teenagers who are dissatisfied with their bodies. Teenagers are very vulnerable to having a negative body image. Around half of all teenage girls think they're 'too fat' and almost 50% of them are dieting or skipping meals to change their weight. Around a quarter of young men aged 16 to 19 are trying to gain weight at any one time.

Reflection

Many women who look in the mirror do not see an accurate reflection. In some studies, up to 80% of women see themselves as larger than they really are. This can be a risk factor for eating disorders. Men tend to judge their body shape more accurately.

Girls as young as six and seven admit to going on diets because they feel 'fat and unattractive', even though many of them are a normal weight or underweight. Children appear to be aware of weight issues at a younger age, compared to twenty years ago. Many countries worldwide have also seen a rise in the number of young people seeking help for eating disorders in the last five years.

It's not surprising that many children and adults are concerned about their appearance, and want to look 'attractive'. Good-looking adults seem to get more advantages in life, such as better chances of gaining a job at interview, or better salaries. As children and teenagers, the good-looking may also get more encouragement from their teachers, and be more popular with their classmates.

Human beings tend to have an irrational belief that physically attractive people are 'good'. If someone looks beautiful or handsome, we are more likely to assume that they have other attractive characteristics, such as intelligence, confidence, social skills, and even high moral values and behaviour. Look at many fairytales and movies, and you will often see that the good guys (Cinderella, Snow White, Peter Pan, Dorothy in *The Wizard of Oz*, Luke Skywalker in *Star Wars*, and so on) look young and attractive, and the bad guys are unattractive, old or disfigured (The Ugly Sisters, The Wicked Stepmother, Captain Hook, The Wicked Witch of the West, Darth Vader under his mask).

Halo effect

Some research suggests that a child's appearance may have an effect on how he or she is treated at school.

This tendency to think the best of attractive people was called the 'Halo Effect' by psychologist Karen Dion, who ran a series of experiments to see how it worked. She told teachers that children had been disruptive and badly behaved in the classroom, then showed the teachers a picture either of an attractive child or of an unattractive child. Teachers who saw the picture of an attractive child were more likely to excuse them, and teachers who saw an unattractive child were more likely to call them 'brats' and blame them. There is also an irrational belief that people who are overweight are stupid and lazy and have no self-control. Studies of the personalities of overweight people have shown that this is not the case. We need to forget our prejudices and look beyond surface appearances.

2 Shape and size
Body fat, body build and fitness

Eating a balanced diet and taking regular exercise can make a big difference to your general health and looks. Sometimes people abuse food, exercise and drugs, in order to change their appearance, so it's important to know what is healthy and what is not.

Healthy eating

A healthy diet includes regular balanced meals, containing nutrients from all the major food groups. Humans need to eat a whole variety of different foods to stay in good condition. There are no 'bad' individual foods, so long as the overall diet is healthy, so you should not feel that you have to deliberately cut anything out. Just keep sugary or fatty foods as occasional treats. Many people skip breakfast, but it is an important meal, boosting the metabolism and helping you to feel more awake and alert in the morning. As lifestyles have become busier, more people have turned to fast food and convenience food for most of their meals. These often contain too much salt, sugar, or fat overall. It's good to know about the basic nutrients in foods, to help you plan a balanced food intake.

⊚ Carbohydrates

Carbohydrates include starchy foods and sugars. Examples of starchy foods are bread, rice, pasta, oats and maize, and they are broken down into sugars when they are digested in the body. Sugars are found naturally in foods

What do you choose?

Knowing the basic facts about food types helps you make healthy choices about what to eat.

like fruit, honey and milk, but can also be added to foods in the form of sucrose, which is processed from sugar cane or sugar beet.

The main function of carbohydrates is to give us energy, and most of them are broken down in the body to make glucose (sometimes called 'blood sugar' when it is circulating around the body in the blood). Dieticians and nutritionists say that we should get most of our energy from carbohydrates, especially unrefined starchy foods such as wholemeal (wholewheat) bread or brown rice, which release their energy slowly and steadily into the body in a healthy way. Generally speaking, highly refined and processed versions of these foods, such as white bread or pasta, contain less fibre and natural vitamins and minerals, and can cause sharp rises in blood sugar.

Sportspeople eat diets rich in carbohydrates to help them train harder and to avoid feeling tired too quickly. It is healthier to get most of your energy from starchy food, and keep sugary sweet foods and drinks for occasional treats. Diets high in sugar can cause tooth decay.

200 calories

Calories

Our food provides us with energy, to drive all the physical and chemical processes of our bodies and to move our muscles. The amount of energy in foods is measured in calories or joules, and the number of calories you need depends on your height, build, age, sex and level of physical activity. As a rough guide, teenage girls need 2,200 calories per day and teenage boys need 2,800 per day.

95 calories

350 calories

385 calories per pint

50 calories

Some of the energy from our food is stored by the body in fat molecules, ready to be used when needed. If we take in more energy (more calories) than we use up, our fat stores increase and we put on weight. If we take in less energy (fewer calories) than we use up, the fat is broken down and we lose weight.

80 calories per slice

⬤ Protein

Protein is made up from smaller units called amino acids. There are many different amino acids, some of which can be made by the body and some of which are 'essential' and must come from the diet. Foods that provide all the essential amino acids include meat, poultry, fish, eggs and dairy products. Foods containing fewer amino acids include pulses (beans and lentils), rice, bread and corn.

Proteins are used by the body to grow and to repair tissues, and to help the immune system. Western diets are very rich in protein, so deficiency is unlikely. You do not need to increase your protein intake unless you are exercising for more than one hour per day.

⬤ Fats and oils

Fats and oils are often described as 'bad' or 'unhealthy', but they are essential in a healthy diet. Fats are found in the walls of every cell in the body, serve as an energy store, and act as padding to protect our internal organs. Fats in the diet come in three main types: poly-unsaturated (sunflower oil, corn oil), mono-unsaturated (olive oil), and saturated (butter, lard) and it's healthiest to eat small and roughly equal amounts of each of them. Oily fish such as salmon and mackerel contain special omega-3 oils which may protect against arthritis, heart disease and mood swings. Fats and oils also carry essential fat-soluble vitamins such as Vitamins A, D and E.

Fats can be unhealthy if they are eaten in very large amounts, and they can be hidden in fried foods, pastries and some dairy products. Just small portions of fat are very high in calories. Diets high in total fat, or high in saturated fats, have been linked to fatty deposits in the blood vessels and heart disease.

Meal plan
Pasta, a bread roll, fish with carrots and kiwi fruits: this meal was designed at a weight loss clinic, to be low in fat and energy while providing essential vitamins, proteins and minerals.

⊛ Vitamins and minerals

Vitamins and minerals, such as iron and calcium, are essential to health and are found in small amounts in all kinds of different foods. Teenagers are sometimes lacking in iron, which is needed to make red blood cells. Iron is found in red meat, and in smaller amounts in fortified breakfast cereals and green vegetables. Calcium is essential for strong bones and teeth, and dairy products are a rich source of this mineral.

Important vitamins and minerals

NAME	FOUND IN	NEEDED FOR
Vitamin A	Beef liver, sweet potato, carrots, butternut squash	Growth, immune system, healthy eyes
Vitamin B complex	Yeast, egg, pork, chicken, cheese, steak, potato, asparagus, salmon, banana	Healthy heart, nerves, muscle, skin, blood cells and pregnancy
Vitamin C	All fruits and vegetables such as papaya, oranges, broccoli, bell peppers	General wellbeing and energy, healthy mouth and gums, fast healing
Vitamin D	Egg yolk, oily fish, also made by human skin exposed to sunlight	Healthy bones, helping the body absorb calcium
Vitamin E	Vegetable oils, wheat germ, poultry, fish	Nerves, muscles and blood, protecting cells
Iron	Red meat, liver, fortified cereals and bread, peas, spinach	Carrying oxygen via the blood, energy reactions inside cells
Calcium	Milk and dairy products, sardines, greens, dried fruit	Strong bones and teeth, muscle movement
Zinc	Oysters, turkey, chicken, whole grains, liver	Energy reactions, growth, healing, removal of toxins

⊛ Dietary fibre

Fibre is found in fruits, vegetables and grains. It is a bulky substance that passes through the body without being digested, and helps to keep the bowel healthy. Diets low in fibre tend to cause constipation, and may be linked to bowel cancer and other problems. Eating five portions of fruit and vegetables every day means that the diet will naturally be high in fibre, and eating unrefined carbohydrates, such as brown rice and wholemeal bread, helps too. Remember to drink enough water to help the fibre pass through the gut.

◉ *Fluids*

Although humans can survive for days without food, they cannot last very long without water, especially in hot weather. We need to drink around six to eight glasses of water daily to replace water lost by sweating, and to flush waste products through our kidneys. Sugary soft drinks, alcohol and drinks containing caffeine, such as coffee and strong tea, can all stimulate the body to lose water, so they are not good to have if you are thirsty.

Water level
Keeping up the level of water in our bodies is vitally important for our health.

Obesity

Many people become overweight in countries where food is cheap and plentiful, especially if they do not take any exercise. Body mass index (BMI) is a simple way to check if someone is in the right range of body weight for their height. Your BMI is your weight (in kg), divided by the square of your height. For example, if you have a weight of 65kg and a height of 1.73m, your BMI will be 65 divided by (1.73 x 1.73) = 21.7 (within the normal range).

BMI takes into account the fact that there are many different body builds, so there is no specific ideal weight for any particular height. As a general rule, a healthy weight for most people means that they have a BMI between 20 and 25, although some people may be slightly outside this range. If they are overweight, they have a BMI between 25 and 30. BMIs over 30 are described as obese, and obese people have a larger proportion of body fat than average. Obesity can lead to many health problems, such as high blood pressure, diabetes, heart disease, certain cancers and arthritis.

The World Health Report 2002 estimated that more than 2.5 million deaths around the world each year are weight-related, and that this is likely to rise. About 320,000 deaths per year in Europe and 300,000 deaths per year in the USA are directly related to obesity. In the UK, adult obesity rates have tripled over the last 20 years. Currently, 19% of adult Britons are obese, and 39% are overweight. Around 17% of British 15-year-olds are now obese. According to the *American Journal of Clinical Nutrition* in June 2002, around 25% of children in the USA have become obese, and 30% of American adults are said to be obese too.

Childhood obesity
This nine-year-old girl is having her blood pressure checked as part of a research project into childhood obesity being carried out at a hospital in Hong Kong.

Exercise for life
Enjoying exercise is an important part of keeping weight under control.

Slightly overweight children and teenagers generally have few immediate health problems, but they may be dissatisfied with their body image, and could be storing up health problems for later in life. Many young people lose excess weight by the time they reach adulthood, due to growth spurts and changes in behaviour. Similarly, underweight or 'gangly' teenagers often fill out to a healthy weight by their mid-twenties. Combating obesity is best done by taking regular, moderate exercise, and changing eating habits to a more healthy and balanced diet. This way, a person uses up more energy than they take in from food, and they do not store the extra energy (calories or joules) as fat. Weight loss is more likely to be successful if it happens slowly over a period of time, and if a person changes their eating habits for good.

Dangerous diets?

The diet industry is big business. In the USA alone, more than $50 billion is spent each year on diet books, programmes, drinks, special foods, pills, gadgets, injections, and more. While some of these products can bring about safe and long-term weight loss, others do not work at all, and some of them are very dangerous. Products are sometimes marketed with false claims, so it's important to read the small print in advertisements, and think about whether

'I weigh too much for my height, but my Mom says I don't need to go on a diet. She says the whole family is going to eat more healthily from now on and I'll probably just grow out of it.'
(Bill, aged 13)

their claims are realistic. Many diets and weight loss products claim to give a 'miracle result' or be a 'quick fix', which appeals to people who feel desperate or bad about themselves. In reality, there are no quick fixes, and although some extreme diets and pills appear to work in the short term, the weight is usually regained quite fast. It has been estimated that 90% of people who crash diet (lose weight rapidly) will put the weight back on, or weigh even more, within 12 months.

Crash diets don't work because they shock the body into a state of starvation. There is usually a rapid loss of weight in the first week of a crash diet, but this is actually only sugar and water being lost, rather than fat. After the first few days, the body reacts to starvation by using up stores of both fat and muscle, while adapting itself to get by on fewer calories. When the person starts eating normally again, their body reacts to the extra calories by storing more of them as fat. So they have gained fat, and lost muscle tone. Even if their weight goes back to the original figure, they will look less toned, and feel more 'flabby'. Many people are then tempted to go on another diet plan, and diet on and off for years. This is a strain on the body and the skin, and is sometimes called yo-yo dieting because weight goes up and down.

'I am always on a diet, it's all I seem to talk about. Some of the people I work with have started avoiding me at lunch times.'
(Laura, aged 18)

Faddy diets go in and out of fashion. They are often diets based around a single food, such as cabbage, peanuts, or grapefruit. They cause short-term weight loss because they cut down on the calories that would normally be eaten – and not, as they may claim, because the single foods have 'special fat-burning' properties. Many of these diets are lacking in vitamins and minerals, and can have all kinds of unhealthy effects. For example, in the 1970s a number of deaths from heart problems were linked to a high-protein drink diet. Teenagers in particular should be careful to avoid crash diets and faddy diets, because they are still growing, and may have high energy needs.

Many females, and an increasing number of males, are utterly obsessed with their food intake. They have a strong fear of becoming fat, think about food all the time, and watch everything they eat. Being watchful all the time takes the fun out of eating, and also makes eating out or going to social occasions very difficult. Although this kind of chronic dieting is not classed as an eating disorder, it has much in common with illnesses such as anorexia and bulimia, and can make life completely miserable.

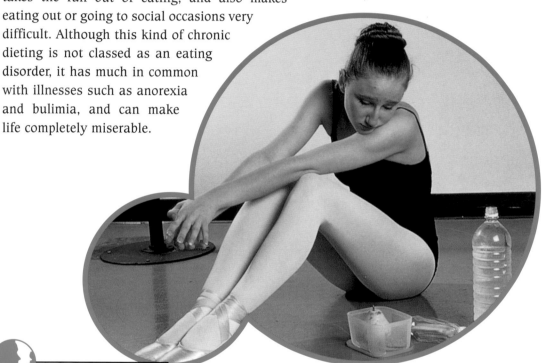

Ellen's story

'I did a lot of dancing. From the age of four I was in a leotard most days, and was very conscious of my body. I remember getting upset about my tummy when I was six. I thought I had a pot belly, although it was actually a normal size. My Mum had a drink problem and didn't seem to enjoy food, and by the age of 12 I had taken control of my own meals and started teaching myself all about calories. I measured my whole worth as a person by my weight, and gradually cut down my food intake until I weighed six stone. I wasn't thinking straight. I got paranoid about eating half an apple. It was a tremendous battle of will against my body, and eating was letting myself down. I was tired all the time and couldn't keep up at dance class. Although people made remarks about me being skinny, nobody mentioned the word "anorexia" or tried to get me to a doctor. Things were getting really serious, and I knew I couldn't carry on, so I allowed myself to put some weight back on, which was very difficult. That kept me out of hospital, but I still worry about my appearance all the time.'
(Ellen, aged 16)

Anorexia nervosa

Anorexia nervosa is an eating disorder that is most common in girls in their mid-teens, although it can affect boys and adults too. Features of anorexia are:

- weight loss of 25% or more of body weight (or having a body weight 25% below normal for age and height);
- distorted body image, so that a grossly underweight person sees themselves as normal or fat;
- avoiding high-calorie foods;
- loss of periods for three months or more (or loss of sexual interest if the person is a teenage or adult male);
- refusal to maintain body weight at or above a minimally normal weight for age and height;
- intense fear of gaining weight or becoming fat.

People with anorexia are obsessed about food, often preparing elaborate meals for friends or family, but not joining in when the meal is eaten. They may develop rituals around eating, such as cutting food into tiny pieces to eat slowly. They may hide their weight loss with baggy clothing, and, if asked, deny that there is a problem. Often, they do not believe that their behaviour is unhealthy. As well as dieting, they may also exercise very hard, or take drugs such as laxatives to lose more weight.

'Back when I was skipping meals and going out running for two hours most days, I would have laughed if anyone suggested I had an eating disorder. I thought only girls had anorexia.'
(Antonio, aged 19)

Many people with anorexia nervosa are described as hard workers, ambitious, or perfectionists. They sometimes say that they are looking for a sense of control over their lives. Long-term starvation causes low blood pressure, dizziness or faintness, a constant feeling of coldness, exhaustion, growth of downy hair (laguno) on the arms and body, and a slowed heartbeat. There can also be stomach pains, constipation and feelings of depression and despair. Over time, the lack of nutrients can lead to the heart muscle and other internal organs being damaged, or osteoporosis (thinning bones). Anorexia can lead to a premature death.

Treatment

Treatment for anorexia usually has two elements: helping the person to regain their normal weight, and counselling. If they have lost more than a certain amount of weight, they are usually admitted to hospital. Re-feeding to increase weight is done slowly to begin with, to allow the body a chance to get used to food again. If weight loss is very severe, the person may need to be fed by tube.

Because many people with anorexia truly do not believe that there is anything wrong with their physical state, it can be very difficult to get them to start eating healthily again. Counselling and therapy can help to combat poor body image, low self-esteem and other personal problems. Family therapy is also helpful. It can take many years to recover from anorexia, and a few people who have the condition never regain their health, or may die. It is thought that the sooner someone gets help for his or her anorexia, the easier it is for them to make a full recovery.

Bulimia nervosa

Bulimia is most often seen in women in their late teens and early twenties, although men are sometimes affected and may rely on excessive exercise to keep their weight down. People with bulimia binge on food: up to 15,000 calories are eaten in one sitting – usually high-calorie foods such as chocolate, ice cream, biscuits and cakes. Afterwards, the person tries to get rid of the extra calories by 'purging' (for example, making themselves vomit) or by taking excessive exercise, and then may go on a strict diet. Many people have bulimia-like symptoms, but for a doctor to diagnose the condition, there must be:

- bouts of binge eating at least twice weekly for three months or longer;
- lack of control over eating during a binge;
- deliberate vomiting, laxative abuse, excessive exercise or fasting after binges;
- body weight mainly within normal limits.

Beating bulimia

Sacha had been dieting hard since the age of sixteen, and never felt thin enough. Whenever she reached her target weight, she would set herself a lower one. All she could think about was food, and she was bad-tempered and snappy. Sacha dreamed about her 'forbidden' foods such as cakes, biscuits and ice cream at night, and craved and fantasized about them during the day. She was constantly fighting herself and ashamed, but yearned for comfort.

One day she decided to allow herself to eat these forbidden foods, and then get rid of them afterwards by vomiting. It seemed a good idea at the time but quickly took over her life like an addiction. She says it was her way of coping with any negative feeling or event, even though she now knows it was an unhealthy reaction.

Soon she was vomiting as many as ten times every day, often bringing up blood. She binged on cakes, cereals and milk, and hid bin bags full of food in her bedroom. It made her secretive and deceptive, and she was able to hide her illness for months, but eventually broke down and told her father. Sacha had counselling and anti-depressants, and had to take a year off school. She says it took her two years to recover.

Over time, deliberate vomiting can lead to stomach acid damaging the enamel on teeth, and to enlarged glands (the parotid glands) on either side of the face. Severe vomiting can upset the person's metabolism and the balance of minerals and fluids in their body and these changes can result in irregular heartbeat, kidney damage and occasionally even death. Laxative abuse can cause stomach bloating and pains, or long-term constipation or diarrhoea.

People with bulimia may have suffered from anorexia when they were younger, or have been teased or bullied for being overweight as a child. They may base their entire sense of self-worth on their body shape or weight. Although they are often described as popular or successful by their friends, people with bulimia tend to feel unworthy or lack self-confidence. They often show signs of being depressed. Because they tend to be secretive about bingeing and purging, and their weight seems normal, their bulimia can be hidden from the people around them.

Treatment

Treatment is normally given on an outpatient basis, but sometimes someone with bulimia needs to be hospitalized if they are very depressed. Cognitive behaviour therapy (CBT) is the most common form of treatment, designed to give the person more understanding about when they binge and why. They are asked to keep a diary of thoughts, feelings and times of binges, and are set tasks aimed at helping them to cope in a positive way in situations where they might be tempted to binge. They may also need advice from a dietician, or treatment for depression.

'Some of the girls in my class go on diets together, and joke about throwing up after meals. I don't see what's so funny about that.' (Prithi, aged 15)

Compulsive eating

This is probably the most common eating problem in men. Men appear to make up about half of all compulsive eaters, although it's hard to guess how many people are affected because they rarely seek help for it. Many people who eat in this way end up becoming obese. Compulsive eaters may 'comfort eat' to cheer themselves up, nibble food all day (this is known as grazing), or have food binges. The binges are similar to those of bulimia, but without the 'purging' after eating.

Compulsive eating often happens as a response to feeling unhappy, bored, lonely or upset. It is a temporary way of blotting out unpleasant feelings. Compulsive eating can also be triggered by long periods of dieting.

Binge eating disorder (BED)

Binge eating disorder (BED) has a specific set of features, although many people who binge eat do not fit into this pattern. The features of BED are:

- *food binges on average twice per week or more, for at least six months;*
- *feeling unable to control eating behaviour during a binge;*
- *feeling unhappy, depressed, or guilty about the binges.*

Unable to stop

A compulsive eater feels unable to stop eating, even though they are not hungry.

Treatment

In a similar way to treatment for bulimia, someone who is a compulsive over-eater can have counselling or therapy. They are often asked to keep a diary about sensations in their bodies, their feelings and the times and nature of binge eating episodes. They are encouraged to work out what triggers their behaviour, and to find more positive ways to express themselves and deal with unhappy feelings. Also, the therapist may encourage them to get back in touch with their natural sensations of hunger, and to recognize if they are full or not after a meal. The emphasis is on eating balanced, regular meals, rather than going on a diet to lose weight.

Healthy exercise

Between 70 and 80% of us are not getting enough exercise. The American College of Sports Medicine and the Health Development Agency in the UK suggest that we should build up to doing around 30 minutes of moderate exercise most days of the week. This can be as simple as going out for a brisk walk, just fast enough to make you breathe slightly deeper and feel as though you're doing some work. How fit you become depends on how many times you exercise each week, how hard you make your muscles work and how long each exercise session lasts. You don't have to be super-fit to get health benefits from being active. Every little counts.

Exercise to suit you

Going out rollerblading is just one way that you could choose to increase the amount of exercise you take.

Regular moderate exercise is good for toning up the body, improving co-ordination and balance, reducing the chance of obesity and decreasing stress and depression. It may protect against heart disease. It can also strengthen growing bones and muscles, be great fun, bring a sense of achievement and lead to new friendships. It isn't all about school exercise lessons or sweating it out in the gym: you can try team games, running, swimming, martial arts, gymnastics, dance, ice-skating, rock climbing, and more. Being more active can also include walking or cycling instead of going by car or bus. The trick to sticking with regular exercise is to find an activity that you really enjoy.

When starting a fitness programme, don't overdo it at the beginning. Ease into it slowly, perhaps starting with three 30-minute sessions per week; then build it up. Speak to your family doctor first if you have any health conditions. Remember to warm up properly before exercise by

'I used to be a bit of a couch potato, but last year I decided to get fitter. Now I cycle to school and back every day and I can really feel the difference. I have lots more energy.'
(Alex, aged 14)

stretching, and then gently increase your activity level and heart rate. Warm down afterwards by slowing down, then doing more stretching.

Compulsive exercising

Some people who take lots of exercise get hooked on the feelings it produces, or the effects it has on their body. It has been estimated that up to 20% of adults who use gyms are compulsive exercisers. They work their bodies too hard, train when they have injuries, and don't rest enough between exercise sessions. Some people with this problem may be using exercise as a way of keeping their minds off personal problems.

Steroid abuse

Anabolic steroids and other drugs might seem a tempting short cut to a 'gym body', but there are many health risks involved, and the drugs can also have unpleasant effects on appearance. Around half of the people who try steroids are teenagers, and just over half of them say that their main reason for doing so is to change their appearance. It has been estimated that 4% of college students use these drugs. Their action in the body is very similar to that of the male hormone testosterone, but the drugs are taken in doses often hundreds of times higher than natural hormone levels.

Taking anabolic steroids has some wanted and some unwanted effects. Steroids seem to make muscle cells retain more protein than usual, so muscles stay larger after exercise. Recovery after exercise is faster and body fat is reduced. Unwanted effects include raised blood pressure and blood cholesterol, increased risk of heart disease and stroke, fluid retention, kidney and liver damage, and damage to bones and joints. There is often increased acne (spots), head hair loss in men and women, growth of breast tissue in men, loss of breast tissue in women, and permanent facial hair and skin coarsening in women.

'Feel-good'

Exercise gives you a boost. It is partly because you release 'feel-good' chemicals called endorphins during, and shortly after, physical activity. Exercise also improves co-ordination and makes you feel more in touch with your body. It helps you to tone up, and can bring a sense of achievement too.

Injecting steroids with dirty needles can spread diseases such as hepatitis B or HIV (the AIDS virus), and injecting into veins can cause gangrene or abscesses. Many drugs sold as steroids are fakes, and may be contaminated with bacteria or other toxins. Psychological effects of taking steroids include increased feelings of energy and motivation, but can swing to unpleasant levels of irritability, aggression, anxiety and depression. This can become extreme aggression, or 'roid rage', where the person loses their temper at the slightest thing and becomes uncontrollably violent. There are mood swings, confusion, problems concentrating and difficulty sleeping, or nightmares.

Anabolic steroids
People who go to the gym or play sport may be offered drugs to help them build up their strength and perform better. These drugs have unpleasant and dangerous side effects.

Muscle dysmorphia

Muscle dysmorphia is sometimes called 'reverse anorexia' or 'bigorexia'. People who suffer from this condition think that they have underdeveloped muscles, when the reverse is actually true. They often work out heavily, and may be tempted to abuse anabolic steroids. Men who have muscle dysmorphia tend to think that they look underweight or weak and small, and women with this condition tend to think they look flabby and untoned. It is not known why people develop this problem, but it has sometimes been linked to bullying, physical attacks and sexual abuse.

Body dysmorphic disorder (BDD)

This may also be called 'imagined ugliness disorder'. Up to 1% of people may have BDD, imagining wrongly that they have some kind of terrible physical defect. They often say that their nose is too big, their hair is too curly, or their skin is too pale, and may go to extreme lengths to correct these 'defects'. They may spend hours looking into mirrors or trying to disguise their appearance, and may seek cosmetic surgery. Treatment includes cognitive behaviour therapy and sometimes anti-depressant medication.

3 Skin deep
On the surface

The surface appearance of the body is easier to change than body shape, and can make a strong first impression. Trying different styles with hair and make-up is fun, and can be an interesting way to express your personality. This chapter explores some of the 'surface' ways in which people choose to change their looks.

It also looks at skin problems such as acne and eczema. Because these are often clearly visible at first glance, they can cause embarrassment or other emotional distress and so have a big effect on a person's body image.

Changing our looks
⚙ Hair

The way a person wears their hair can be a way of showing what gang they belong to, their taste in music or their beliefs. In the fashion world, hairstyles change from season to season, with different colours and shapes, styling products and accessories. Experimenting with hairstyles can be a good way to work out what flatters your face or suits your personality best. The more hair is altered from its natural colour and style, the more it can become damaged or out of condition, so it's important to treat it gently if you change your look frequently.

⚙ Cosmetics and skin

Men and women have been using cosmetics for centuries to temporarily change their appearances. For example, ancient

Experimenting
It is fun to try out new styles and colours and see how they suit your personality.

Egyptians used kohl, a dark pigment, to make their eyes look larger. Mass production in the twentieth century brought the price of cosmetics down, and now there's a wide range of products available from fake tan to false eyelashes.

Many people with white/Caucasian skin like to tan in the sun or on sun-beds, but this can cause young people to start getting wrinkles at an early age, and is a big risk factor for skin cancer. Wearing a high-factor sunscreen, such as factor 20, and avoiding intense midday sunlight are strongly advised to reduce this risk. People with darker skin are sometimes tempted to use skin lightening products, but these can make the skin tone uneven or patchy and can cause burns. Skin colour is often safest and at its most beautiful when it is left to nature.

'I wear lots of eyeliner – it's part of my look. Most people wouldn't recognize me if they saw me without my make-up.' (Kim, aged 16)

◉ Body modification

Body modification includes tattooing, piercings, scarification (deliberate scarring) and branding. Any of these can make a strong visual statement, and be individual, interesting, or shocking. Tattoos were first given in the Polynesian Islands, for religious and 'coming of age' reasons, and were done slowly and painfully by hand. They became popular with Western

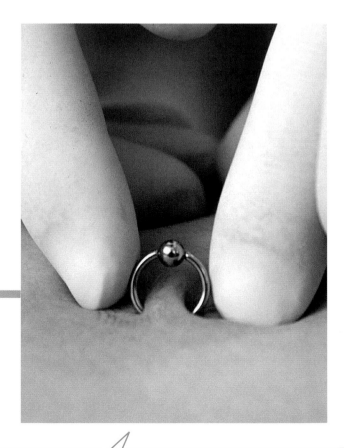

Painstaking process
Like some other ways in which people choose to modify their appearance, having a piercing involves some pain.

Tips to look your best

Looking healthy is cheaper than most people think. In fact, some of the simplest things you can do are free. They have very little to do with brand names, fashion, or expensive gym memberships.

- *Avoid cigarettes: smoking is bad for overall health, causes lines and wrinkles, and robs the body of nutrients like Vitamin C.*
- *Wear sunscreen and avoid sunburn.*
- *Eat healthily: it's good for hair, bones, skin and growth.*
- *Exercise: it gives a glow to the skin and helps you to tone up.*
- *Accept yourself: dress to suit your body type.*
- *Get enough sleep: it's good for general wellbeing and bright eyes.*
- *Look after teeth: visit the dentist regularly, and brush twice a day to keep stains, gum disease and tooth decay at bay.*

sailors and royalty, but were not common among ordinary Westerners until after a tattooing machine was invented in 1891.

Piercing is popular now but has been around for hundreds of years: nose and lip ornaments have been found in Inca burial grounds. Most countries have age limits and hygiene standards for tattooing and piercing parlours. Disposable needles and sterilized equipment must be used to prevent the spread of bacteria and viruses such as hepatitis and HIV.

'Think carefully if you want a tattoo. They can be removed, but results are not perfect, and the process can be painful and expensive, and require several treatments. Tattoos can also give people the wrong idea about you.'
(Sarah, aged 18)

Tattoos are difficult and expensive to remove, often taking several sessions of laser therapy before they fade, and possibly leaving scarring or uneven colouring of the skin. Piercings are relatively easy to take out in most cases, but can leave permanent holes behind.

Acne

Acne, also called spots or zits, tends to happen for the first time in the teenage years. Most teens have the occasional acne spot or two, but others can have moderate or severe acne with many blackheads, whiteheads, spots and sometimes scarring. It usually appears on the face, but can also crop up on the chest, back and neck. Although having acne doesn't bother everyone, many people say that it makes them feel down, ashamed, or lacking in self-confidence.

'My acne got so bad I didn't want to leave the house. My Mum was really supportive and took me to the dermatologist, after the GP had referred me, and now my skin is finally clearing up.'
(Tom, aged 16)

Stressful life events and increases in the hormone testosterone often trigger the start of acne. Males produce much more testosterone than females, so they tend to be more badly affected. Normal skin contains millions of hair follicles, each of which has a tiny sebaceous (oil) gland attached to it. Increased testosterone makes the sebaceous glands produce much more oil, so the follicles become more easily blocked. The blockage contains skin pigments, so it appears black (a 'blackhead'), but it is made up of oil and skin cells, not dirt. Whiteheads are small, pale-coloured spots, about the same size as blackheads, which contain the same material without the pigment. Oil and bacteria build up around the follicles, causing inflammation and larger spots. Sometimes a follicle ruptures, and this leads to more inflammation and cysts (sacs of pus) under the skin.

Myth

Eating certain foods, such as chocolate, causes acne.

Fact

Chocolate does not cause acne and small amounts are fine, but eating a balanced diet with plenty of fruit and vegetables can be good for general wellbeing of the skin.

Treatment

Mild acne, with only the occasional spot, can usually be kept in check by using simple anti-bacterial washes and cleansing products. Many preparations contain benzoyl peroxide, which has an anti-bacterial action and reduces the number of whiteheads. Some people find it dries or irritates their skin. Other preparations contain salicylic acid, or tea tree oil in dilute form. It is usually a case of trying something for a few weeks to see if it suits you.

Moderate acne, where there are many spots that are resistant to simple creams and washes, can be treated with medicines prescribed by your family doctor. Antibiotics are usually prescribed as tablets, or applied directly to the skin. They can take eight weeks to start working, and treatment generally continues for six months or more. Certain brands of contraceptive pill may be prescribed to reduce acne in some young women.

Severe acne causes scarring, and can affect large areas of skin. A dermatologist (skin specialist) can prescribe powerful medications including retinoids and antibiotics. Retinoids are similar to Vitamin A, and may be given in tablet or cream form to reduce inflammation and scarring, and regulate oil production.

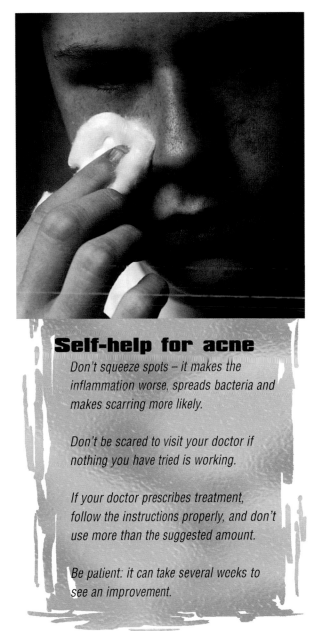

Self-help for acne

Don't squeeze spots – it makes the inflammation worse, spreads bacteria and makes scarring more likely.

Don't be scared to visit your doctor if nothing you have tried is working.

If your doctor prescribes treatment, follow the instructions properly, and don't use more than the suggested amount.

Be patient: it can take several weeks to see an improvement.

As with many other skin problems, people can be ignorant about the causes of acne, and may make hurtful or unhelpful comments. For example, they may wrongly think that all cases of acne are caused by being dirty and not washing enough, when most of the time this isn't true.

Eczema

About one in eight children, and one in 12 adults suffer from eczema (dermatitis). Areas of skin become very dry, itchy and flaky. The skin can also be reddened, sore, inflamed, or weepy. It tends to affect areas such as the elbows, wrists, hands, face and backs of the knees. The itchiness can keep the person awake, and make them feel irritable. Teenagers often say that they feel very awkward or embarrassed when their eczema flares up. Over time, if eczema is not treated, itching and scratching can lead to thickening and hardening of the skin.

The most common types of eczema are atopic eczema and contact eczema. Atopic eczema tends to run in families and develop during childhood. People often grow out of it as they get older, but may also suffer from hayfever or asthma. Illness or certain foods may make their eczema worse. Contact eczema tends to happen in teens or adults, and is caused by contact with an irritant such as nickel, soap, perfume, or glue.

Treatment

There is no 'cure' for eczema, but there are many ways to keep it in check and prevent it from flaring up again. It's important to stop the skin from drying out, so using only gentle, soap-free cleansers and applying emollient (moisturizing) creams and lotions helps. Steroid creams can be used on patches of eczema during a flare-up, to bring down the inflammation, but should only be used in tiny amounts and for short periods as they can cause thinning of the skin if over-used. Antihistamines may be prescribed to reduce the itching and to help sleep at night. They block the effects of histamine, a chemical that causes irritation during allergic reactions. For the most severe cases of eczema, a doctor can prescribe steroid tablets and other medication.

Eczema self-help

- However hard it may be, try not to scratch. It makes inflammation worse, and can infect the skin with viruses or bacteria.
- Avoid any known triggers if possible, checking the ingredients carefully when buying products such as shampoo, cosmetics and washing powder.
- Try relaxation techniques to reduce tension, because stress is thought to cause flare-ups in some people.
- Moisturize skin every day.
- During a flare-up, avoid sports that make you very sweaty.
- Wear cotton clothes, and avoid wool and polyester.

To prevent further flare-ups it can be useful to find what the triggers are, and then avoid them. For contact dermatitis, patch tests can be carried out, where small amounts of suspected irritants are applied to the skin to see which have the strongest effects. If someone has atopic eczema, they may need special tests to look for foods or airborne substances that could be causing problems. Some people try alternative treatments such as Chinese herbs, homeopathy and acupuncture. If you are considering these, always use a registered, fully qualified practitioner.

Psoriasis

One in 50 people has psoriasis, and it often starts during the teenage years after sore throats or chest infections, or stressful events such as exams or relationship problems. The exact cause of it is unknown, but it sometimes runs in families. It isn't contagious – in other words, it isn't infectious and cannot spread from person to person.

Psoriasis can appear anywhere on the body, and is most common on the knees, ankles and scalp, or on areas that get bumped or injured. Normal skin cells are renewed every 28 days, but in psoriasis they are replaced every four days, causing 'plaques' where the skin is thicker. Plaques tend to be red or dark pink areas, with a silvery, scaly surface. They can be very uncomfortable and itchy, and often make people feel self-conscious about the way they look.

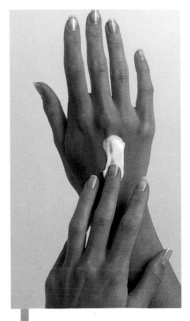

Moisture supply
Keeping skin moisturized with appropriate creams or lotions helps keep the symptoms of eczema and psoriasis at bay.

Treatment

There is no cure for psoriasis at the moment, but it can be kept at bay with treatment. Taking care of general health, and reducing stress levels can help to reduce the number of flare-ups. Keeping skin moisturized reduces itching, and wearing soft cotton clothes reduces skin irritation. To get rid of the plaques, a doctor may prescribe medicines that are similar to Vitamin D, and steroid creams. Sometimes, clinics provide special ultraviolet light treatment, which needs to be carefully monitored.

'If one more person asks me if it's infectious, I think I'm going to scream. No, it's just a tiny bit of psoriasis. It isn't going to hurt anybody.' (Emily, aged 17)

4 Puberty and growth
Changes in young people

Body image is influenced by how we picture ourselves in our minds (including size and shape), the physical sensations we get from our bodies, how we think others see us, and how we feel about our bodies. All of these things can change during puberty and growth, and so overall body image can change too.

There is a wide range of body types, which become more obvious as people grow and mature. This variation is natural and healthy, and makes us unique individuals. There is no 'good' or 'bad' body type. Our type is largely determined by genetics: we usually take after our parents in characteristics such as height and body shape.

Growth

Growth includes height and weight gain. Children grow in response to growth hormone, a hormone produced by the pituitary gland in the brain. Everyone grows at different rates and at different times, but most people fall into the following pattern. Growth is rapid in infants and young children up to the age of three or four. Gains are steady but not so rapid after this, and girls and boys continue to grow at a slower rate. At this point, boys and girls have the same amount of body fat.

Growth spurt

As children become adults at puberty, they experience a growth spurt. The age at which it happens varies, and so there can be big variations between friends.

After this slower growth phase, growth speeds up again for the adolescent 'growth spurt'. This happens earlier in girls, who tend to have their growth spurt between the ages of 10 and 15. Boys usually have their growth spurt between the ages of 12 and 17. In some adolescents, these changes happen very quickly, and in others the changes take a lot longer.

'Sometimes I look around at people and I'm amazed at how we all come in such different shapes and sizes.' (Tanya, aged 15)

At the age of 12, girls are often taller and bigger than boys of the same age. Changes can be noticed in body composition (the amount of muscle, bone, fat, etc). Girls' bodies increase in body fat and muscle, and girls of the same age start to have a wider variation in their weight, height and body shape. Boys' bodies increase in muscle and lose some fat during puberty. For example, muscle can make up about 42% of the body weight of a boy aged 5, but by the time he is 17 his amount of muscle could increase, to make up 54% of his body weight.

By the age of 14, both girls and boys are getting taller and heavier, but the boys are catching up with the girls in height and weight. At this age, some of the group will have had quite a large growth spurt and others will not have. At 16, boys tend to be taller than girls, although some girls will be taller than boys of the same age.

'I've got Sever's disease, where the bones in my legs are growing faster than the tendons in my ankles. It hurts right now, but the doctor says I'll grow out of it soon.' (Kofi, aged 13)

Bones grow in length to contribute to the final height, but not all at the same time. The hands and feet tend to start growing first, followed by arms and legs. The spine is the last area to start having a growth spurt, so the body can look out of proportion or feel ungainly at this time. It can be reassuring to know that it all evens out in the end, even if things feel strange for a while.

Some bones change in shape too at puberty. In males, the shoulders broaden, and in females the hips widen (probably to make giving birth easier when they are adults). After this there are slower increases in bone growth until the adult height and weight are reached, usually between the ages of 18 to 20.

Growth problems

Some teenagers and children are much smaller or much bigger than their classmates, or go through puberty much later or earlier. Many people find that they eventually catch up with their classmates, or that their classmates catch up with them, and it is a temporary situation. In the meantime, looking or feeling 'different' from the people around them can mean that they feel vulnerable or get teased. It can be a great help if they get support and reassurance from parents, teachers and friends.

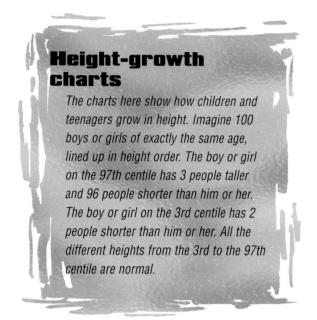

Height-growth charts

The charts here show how children and teenagers grow in height. Imagine 100 boys or girls of exactly the same age, lined up in height order. The boy or girl on the 97th centile has 3 people taller and 96 people shorter than him or her. The boy or girl on the 3rd centile has 2 people shorter than him or her. All the different heights from the 3rd to the 97th centile are normal.

Patterns of growth for boys

The coloured area shows the range of heights that are considered normal for boys at different ages.

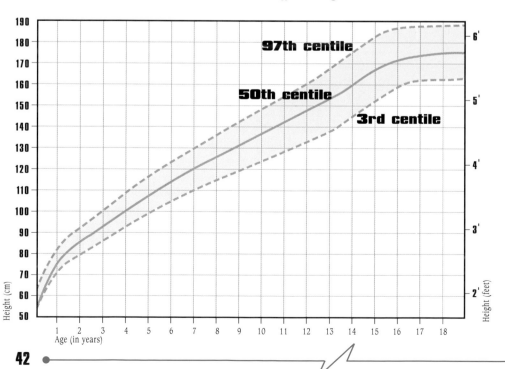

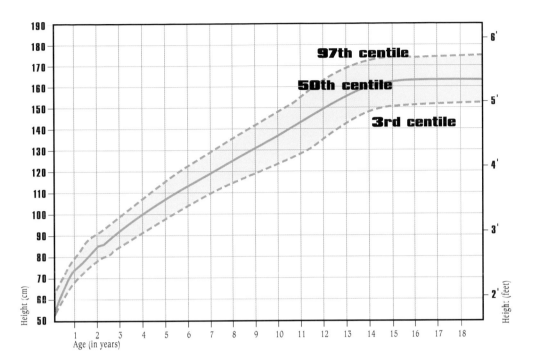

Small for their age

Children and teenagers who are below the third centile on the height-growth chart are small for their age. In babies, this is measured by head circumference, body weight and length of the entire body. Over 80% of the children and teenagers who are small for their age are healthy and are small simply because they take after their parents, who are also small. Doctors sometimes call this 'familial short stature'. Some children, more commonly boys, have a later growth spurt than average, but tend to eventually catch up with their classmates and end up at a normal height. This also tends to run in families, and may be called 'familial growth delay'. Boys in particular may be teased about being shorter than their friends, or feel distressed, but are often reassured when they find out that it is only a temporary problem.

Social deprivation, emotional stress, or a disrupted or unhappy home life can lead to babies or teenagers failing to grow. It is thought that the stress reduces the amount of growth hormone that they produce, which is a major factor

Patterns of growth for girls
The coloured area shows the range of heights that are considered normal for girls at different ages.

in growing taller and gaining weight. The good news is that if the emotional stress is reduced, they can start growing at a normal rate again. Eating disorders can have a serious impact on growth, because children and teens with eating disorders do not get the amount or kinds of nutrients they need to develop. However, simply being a 'picky' eater generally does not have this effect.

There are some genetic problems that can cause short stature. For example, Turner Syndrome, a condition in girls where one of their X-chromosomes is missing, can cause a reduced adult height. Hormone disorders are a relatively rare cause of reduced height, but lack of growth hormone can have strong effects upon growth. Growth hormone deficiency can be treated by giving the young person injections of artificially-produced growth hormone.

Illness can affect growth, especially diseases such as renal (kidney) failure, juvenile arthritis (inflamed joints), cystic fibrosis (long-term infections in the lungs) and intestinal

I hated my height

'I was always the smallest boy in my class, and although it didn't matter much when I was younger, I got more and more self-conscious about it as I went through my early teens. The taller guys in my class sometimes tapped me on the head and called me "shorty", which made me very angry and annoyed. I even got into a couple of fights over it, trying to make a point and look like a tough guy I suppose. The school told my parents, and I was so embarrassed. They took it quite well though – I was surprised. My Dad's short himself, and he took me to one side and explained that even though he isn't the tallest man in the world, he has done well for himself, and has great friends and a beautiful wife and kids. I hadn't thought about it like that before, but it made sense, and he is a good role model. I am a bit more relaxed about my height now, which is just as well, because I can't change it.'
(Mike, aged 20)

problems. This is usually because the body isn't absorbing enough nutrients to grow properly, or is using lots of energy to deal with health problems such as infections or inflammation.

Specialist surgery is available for some young people who are very short, and can add up to four inches of height. It is done by breaking and gradually stretching out the thigh bone over several months. The technique is painful, makes mobility difficult for a long time, and there is a risk of infection and brittle bones.

Tall for their age

Most children and teenagers who are tall for their age are perfectly healthy and have inherited their height from their parents. While boys are sometimes upset about being 'too short', girls are sometimes upset about being 'too tall'. Doctors are sometimes asked to treat tall girls to stop them getting any taller, but if someone is healthy and destined to be very tall, it is much safer to avoid interfering with their growth. Sometimes, children who are tall for their age may simply be going through puberty earlier than their friends. A smaller number of very tall children and teenagers produce too much growth hormone, usually because of a tumour in the pituitary gland. Pituitary tumours can be treated with surgery, radiotherapy, or drugs.

Puberty

Puberty is the series of physical changes that turn children into adults capable of reproduction. The emotional and social maturity needed to be ready for sexual relationships, and to cope with pregnancy and raising a child, is reached much later than the physical maturity. This is almost certainly why societies all around the world have rules and laws to prevent sex below a certain age.

Myth

Giving growth hormone to anyone who is below average height will make them taller.

Fact

Most people who are shorter than average simply take after their parents, and giving them growth hormone will make no difference to their final height. If someone is in their very late teens or older, they have stopped growing, so giving them growth hormone will not affect their height either.

Puberty can be a time of rapid change, with alterations to the face, body hair, sexual organs and overall body shape. Some people sail through it, and others have a more bumpy journey. Young people need some time to get used to these changes in the way their bodies look, work and feel. Being the first or last in the class to undergo puberty can be very difficult because it visibly marks someone out as 'different', at a time when they might just want to blend in or be the same as their friends. It helps to understand what's going on, what's 'normal' and what to expect. The process is controlled by a complex system of hormones, some of them produced in the hypothalamus gland in the brain, and some of them produced by the ovaries in females, and the testicles in males.

Girls

Most girls begin puberty between the ages of nine and 13. The first sign is generally breast formation, but sometimes it is the growth of pubic hair. The hair in the underarms also begins to grow thicker and darker, and menstrual periods begin

Finding a style

As they become more independent, teenagers enjoy experimenting with their appearance, but for many it is also important to fit in with the current fashion.

'My body changed quite quickly. For a while I was the only girl in the class with these big hips and thighs, and boobs. It took some time to get used to it.' (Suzy, aged 16)

on average around the age of 12 to 13, although it's not unusual for them to begin as early as the age of nine. Under the influence of the female hormone cycle, an egg is released from the ovary every month, and passes down the fallopian tubes to the uterus (womb). If the egg is not fertilized by sperm, the lining of the womb and some blood are shed as a period, through the vagina. Most girls do not have regular periods to begin with, and may start their periods before they start ovulating (releasing eggs from the ovaries). Once a girl starts ovulating, she is capable of becoming pregnant if she has a sexual relationship.

Boys

Boys begin puberty later than girls, usually between the ages of eleven and 15. The first sign is usually growth of the testicles and scrotum, followed by growth of pubic and underarm hair and the penis. The vocal cords lengthen and the voice becomes deeper. In some boys the voice changes gradually, but in others it can crack or 'break' and it can be hard to control the pitch for a while. Around this time, boys start producing sperm in their testicles. The first ejaculations of semen (sperm mixed with other fluids) begin, and can happen while a boy is asleep (a 'wet dream'). From this time onward, a boy is capable of making a girl pregnant. Facial hair starts to grow thicker and darker, and the penis and testicles continue to grow up to the age of around 18 to 20.

'Everyone noticed when my voice broke. One minute it was all high and squeaky, the next it was deep. I dreaded having to speak in class.'
(Carl, aged 17)

Delayed or early puberty

Some girls and boys may experience early development of breasts or of pubic hair, or they may go through puberty much later or earlier than people the same age. It can cause worry and embarrassment, and a visit to the doctor can be helpful and reassuring.

Delayed puberty may run in the family, and is not always something to worry about. Puberty can also be delayed in young people who are very undernourished, or who have a lack of hormone production in their hypothalamus or sex organs. Turner Syndrome in girls often means that their ovaries are very small or absent, causing a lack of ovarian hormones that start the menstrual cycle. Males who have Klinefelter Syndrome have an extra X-chromosome, and reduced testosterone release from the testicles. Chemotherapy or radiotherapy treatments for young people who have cancer can also lead to delayed puberty.

Around 90% of girls who start puberty very young have no health problems, and it is not something to worry about. Many boys who start puberty early are healthy too, but may need some medical tests as a precaution. Early puberty can be caused by an overactive hypothalamus, tumours of the ovary or testicle, diseases of the adrenal glands (glands found just above the kidney) and intake of synthetic sex hormones.

Social changes

The teenage years are halfway between childhood and adulthood, going from complete dependence on parents to complete independence. They are a time when intense friendships are formed, and although teenagers may want to assert their independence and individuality, they also need to feel part of a gang, and have some parental guidance and support. Many teenagers place a very large part of their self-esteem in their body image, and try to look a certain way, or fit in with a gang. The body is changing dramatically, and it is sometimes hard to know whether the changes are normal, or how someone will finally end up looking. Sometimes the changes are exciting and positive, and sometimes they are a source of anxiety, and teenage is a time when people are very sensitive to comments about their looks and attractiveness.

Part of a gang
Clothes and hairstyle can suggest what gang someone belongs to, or the kind of music they like.

5 Plastic surgery
Cosmetic and medical operations

The number of people opting to have plastic surgery each year has tripled over the last decade. This is partly because techniques have improved, and partly because more people can afford to have cosmetic work done, or feel unhappy about themselves. Surgery is not without serious risks, and should not be entered into lightly. In most cases, cosmetic procedures are highly unsuitable for teenagers, and are not a long-term solution to deal with low self-esteem or confidence.

What is plastic surgery?

Plastic surgery is either reconstructive or cosmetic (also called 'aesthetic'). Where possible, reconstructive surgery aims to restore parts of the body. It is used to help people recover from burns, or from operations or accidents where large amounts of tissue or skin have been removed. For example, it is used after breast cancer surgery. Cosmetic surgery is more to do with people changing parts of their body that they don't like the look of. It is mostly made up of operations to:

- change features that were present at birth, or become more obvious at puberty;
- counteract health problems, such as obesity;
- reverse changes due to the ageing process.

In profile
These photographs were taken before and after plastic surgery to change the shape of a woman's nose.

What operations are most common?

Not all surgeons will carry out cosmetic operations on teenagers, but the most common ones in this age group are nose reshaping and ear surgery. The most common cosmetic procedures in people of all ages include breast augmentation (breast implants), liposuction, nose reshaping, facelifts and eyelid surgery.

Reconstructive surgery is most commonly carried out to cover areas of lost skin or tissue when removing tumours, repair injured hands, reduce breast size (in men and women), reconstruct breasts after cancer treatment, and repair wounds caused by accidents.

In most cases, the operations described below are carried out in hospital under a general anaesthetic, where the patient is completely unconscious. There is a small risk of chest infections or blood clots forming whenever this is used. Any time someone goes under anaesthesia, there is a risk of death, no matter how fit and healthy they are.

Nose reshaping

Nose reshaping is also called rhinoplasty, nasal refinement, or a 'nose job'. The nose can be reshaped by reducing or increasing the size, removing a 'hump' in the middle, or changing the shape of the tip, bridge, or nostrils. To

Duncan's nose

When Duncan was twelve, he got into a big playground fight. He was punched hard in the nose and eye, and noticed afterwards that there was a dent in the side of his nose. As he grew older, the bend in his nose got bigger and bigger, eventually making it impossible to breathe through.

At the age of seventeen, he was accepted for free surgery to straighten it out again, and went in to hospital just before Christmas. After a general anaesthetic, the surgeon broke the bone in Duncan's nose and re-set it. He had plaster on his face for two weeks, and splints sewn inside his nostrils to keep everything in place. He had to put up with pain, black eyes and big nosebleeds. Six months later he had to have a second operation to remove some more cartilage from the inside of his nose, to allow him to breathe more freely through it. Even though he felt terrible at the time, Duncan says it was definitely worth it, and is also amazed at the difference when he looks at old photos.

increase the size of the nose, or to even out dents, an implant (bone, cartilage or synthetic material) may be inserted into the nose. Reducing nose size may involve removing bone, cartilage, or soft tissue. A typical operation lasts one to two hours, and the nose is kept still afterwards with a plaster splint. There is often swelling and bruising around the eyes and the nose, headaches and nosebleeds.

'Bat ear' correction

Up to 2% of the UK population think that their ears stick out too much, and children often say they are teased if they have 'bat ears'. If the problem is clearly visible when a baby is born, the cartilage in the ears can be gently pushed back by splinting, but after six months of age the cartilage hardens and can only be changed by surgery. The surgeon cuts through the skin behind the ear, cuts out some of the cartilage, then stitches the cartilage together so that the ear lies flatter against the head. The ears are then bandaged while they heal.

Hurtful taunts
Class mates can be cruel, making someone feel that they are laughing at their appearance.

Liposuction

This procedure has become popular in recent years, and is carried out to reduce body fat in areas such as the belly, hips, thighs and buttocks. A good surgeon only operates if someone has already tried healthy eating and exercise. Small cuts are made in the skin and fat is sucked out of the tissue underneath with a narrow metal tube. Afterwards there can be pain, swelling, numbness, tingling, bruising or permanent bagginess of the skin and tissues.

'At fourteen, I was desperate to have a boob job, but I was far too young. Now I'm older, I realize that they suit my body best the way they are, and I'm glad I didn't go under the knife as soon as I could.'
(Kate, aged 20)

Breast surgery

The three most common plastic surgery operations on the breasts are reconstruction after breast cancer, breast augmentation (augmentation mammoplasty, breast implants, or a 'boob job') and breast reduction. Implants are bags of silicone gel or sterile oil or salt solution.

Facelifts

The most common age group for a facelift is people in their 50s and 60s, who want to tighten up sagging facial skin. It can take weeks to recover from a facelift, and there are several risks, including damage to facial nerves, infection and bleeding, heavy scarring and change to the hairline.

Non-surgical procedures

The following procedures, which don't involve surgery, are becoming increasingly popular. They sometimes have permanent and dramatic results, and they may go wrong. They should only be carried out by an experienced practitioner.

- *Chemical peels: solutions painted onto facial skin to remove the top layer.*
- *Micro-dermabrasion: sterile crystals blown onto the face at high speed to remove the top layer of skin.*
- *Botox ®: injections of Botulinum toxin to temporarily paralyse facial muscles and smooth out wrinkles.*
- *'Filler' injections: collagen, body fat and other materials, placed under the skin to fill out acne scars, lines or wrinkles.*
- *Laser hair removal: hair follicles are permanently destroyed by using a laser.*

Important things to think about

Anyone thinking about having cosmetic surgery needs to know exactly what they are letting themselves in for. It's important to read about how the operations are done, who they are suitable for, and how long it will take to recover.

- The vast majority of surgeons refuse to carry out cosmetic operations on teenagers who are still growing. Some young people who dislike part of their body find that they 'grow into' their looks. Body image counselling is often much more appropriate.

- Cosmetic surgery can be painful, and recovery can take time. There is often bruising and swelling.

- Results are not always what people wanted, and things can go wrong. General anaesthetics have risks, as do all operations, and there may be complications. Some people do die unexpectedly during cosmetic surgery.

- Having surgery for cosmetic reasons is usually expensive. It's big business and there are some greedy people who are happy to carry out surgery although they are not qualified, are inexperienced, or do not do their jobs properly.

- If you are generally dissatisfied with yourself, changing one part of your body is unlikely to make you happy in the long run.

Cosmetic and reconstructive surgery often has very satisfied customers, and it may give them a confidence boost if it is successful. However, realistically, it's unlikely to help anyone pass exams, get their dream job, or find their perfect partner. It's not a 'magic wand' that makes everything better. Improving general self-esteem and self-confidence may have much more positive effects than going under the knife, and counselling to improve body image may be a much healthier option. Chapter 6 contains several exercises that can help people feel better about the way they look.

The family doctor can advise on whether or not surgery is suitable. They will also be able to explain more about operations, and how surgeons must be registered with the appropriate professional bodies. Asking trusted family and friends if they think surgery would make a positive difference can be useful, provided that they are very sensible, honest and kind. These measures can help to put appearances into perspective.

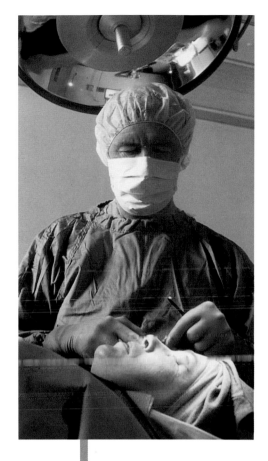

In the theatre
Any operation carries risks, including from the effect of the anaesthetic, used to make the person unconscious.

6 Improving body image
Ways to help yourself and others

Nearly everybody feels down about some aspect of their appearance from time to time. There's no need to worry if you feel like this occasionally. Remember that body image is dynamic: it changes from day to day, and from situation to situation. Sadly, sometimes, a negative body image can be more of a problem.

Signs of a problem

- You constantly compare yourself to others, or put yourself down over your appearance.
- You feel depressed about your body most or all of the time.
- You avoid exercise, the beach, or social situations because of the way you look.
- You hate looking at old photos of yourself or having your picture taken.
- Relatives or friends tease you or make insulting comments about your appearance.
- You spend long periods looking in the mirror every day, or avoid your reflection wherever possible.
- You are constantly on a diet; or crash dieting, putting the weight back on, then starting another crash diet.
- You exercise too hard, and feel guilty or anxious if you miss a single training session. You exercise when you are ill or should be resting.
- You take drugs such as diet pills, laxatives, or anabolic steroids to change the way you look, even though they might make you feel unwell and put your health at risk.
- You obsess about food or cosmetic surgery when everyone you know says that you look fine.

Are any of these signs true of you? If so, you might like to look at the ideas for getting your body image in perspective, or ways to gain a more positive body image, that are listed later in this chapter.

Signs that a friend may be in trouble

- Rapid weight loss or weight gain over a short period of time.
- Avoiding meals, hiding food, or going straight to the toilet after eating.
- Training extra hard for long periods of time, without rest days, or when they have injuries. Acting upset when they can't exercise.
- Being bullied or taunted about some part of their appearance.
- Focusing on one part of their body, saying it needs to be changed or they hate it, especially if they look fine to you.
- Wearing baggy clothes to hide weight loss, or 'small' muscles.
- Talking about looks or food for all or most of the time you spend together.

Is a friend in trouble?

Taking a strong interest in their appearance is quite normal for teenagers, and so are changes in body size or shape. The signs above may show that someone is in trouble, but they can also sometimes be confused with normal teenage changes.

If you are worried about a friend, don't be scared to let them know. Be supportive, and give them time to talk. They may react angrily, or deny that there's anything wrong, or swear you to secrecy. If you are fairly sure that something is wrong and they need help, you may have to make the hard decision to tell someone such as a parent, school nurse, or teacher. The sooner someone gets support or treatment, the sooner they can start to feel better.

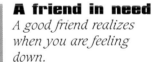

A friend in need
A good friend realizes when you are feeling down.

Being realistic

Instead of taking all your cues from television, magazines and movies, look around more often at real human beings. People of all shapes, sizes, ages and races can be beautiful; there is no one 'perfect' way to be. Beauty is in the eye of the beholder – it's 'all in the mind'. Remember that what is considered attractive now was considered unattractive years ago, and it may change again in the future.

Don't be fooled into thinking that the 'ideal' images in the media represent 'normal' or 'average' people. Modelling agencies and the film industry tend to select people with very unusual body types. The people you see in pictures and on screen represent less than 5% of the population. What is portrayed as 'healthy' in the media is not always so: they tend to have much less body fat than doctors think is healthy, and eating disorders are common.

No matter how hard we try, most of us will not look like models or actors, but that's okay. Even models and actors don't look like models and actors most of the time! For many of them, working on the way they look takes up several hours every day.

Remember that advertisements exist to sell us things – not for any other reason. Some of them deliberately set out to make us feel envious, insecure, or unattractive. A few of them are downright misleading or dishonest.

Media models
Fashion magazines may give you many useful ideas – but they need to be adapted for the real world.

Don't kid yourself. If you were to look a particular way, your life would not become 'perfect'. Don't fall into the trap of thinking that a particular look means that a person has a good personality, is intelligent or successful, or has happy loving relationships. Life just doesn't work like that! None of those qualities depends on physical appearance.

Positive body image

Having a good body image is about feeling comfortable with yourself, liking and caring for yourself. You don't have to change your appearance to gain a better body image; just change the way you think and behave a little.

Remember that your body is not an object or an ornament. It is your home, not your enemy, and it allows you to move and do all kinds of amazing things. Think about how your body functions, and be impressed by all the parts of it that work properly. Celebrate your uniqueness, rather than trying to look the same as everyone else.

Don't weigh yourself every day, and if you spend long periods looking in the mirror, try hiding the mirrors in your house for a week. Try not to measure your appearance against celebrities and other people in the media. If that's very difficult, you could try taking a break from magazines, movies and television for a few days.

If you want to feel better about your body, make friends with it rather than fighting against it, or judging yourself harshly. Take care of your physical and emotional health with regular moderate exercise, healthy eating, rest and relaxation.

Don't smoke cigarettes to try to lose weight: it can give you stained teeth, bad breath, wrinkles, chest infections and an increased risk of lung cancer and heart disease. Avoid crash diets and obsessive exercise.

Stand and look in a mirror for a few minutes, and listen to the thoughts that run through your head. If you find yourself having negative thoughts about the way you look, try to turn them into something more positive. For everything you don't like about your looks, try to think of two things that you do like, even if it's only small things to begin with. Perhaps you like your eyes, smile, toes and so on. Say them out loud or write them down, and look at them from time to time if you feel low.

'I like and respect myself and my body.'

'I am a good person and I deserve the best in life.'

'The way I look is fine. I like the way I look.'

Affirmations

Saying positive phrases to yourself can combat negative thoughts. If you repeat them every day, they will sink in, even if you don't completely believe them at first. You can make up your own affirmations or try one of these.

Talk to people about how you feel, especially if they are kind, honest, positive people. Share your thoughts and experiences with others, such as parents or friends. You can also see a counsellor or therapist who will work with you to help you improve your body image.

'Having counselling was the best thing I ever did. I realized that what I needed to do was change how I felt about myself, not change my body.'
(Amie, aged 17)

Improving self-esteem

Self-esteem is about how much you like yourself, and how good you feel about yourself. Take the emphasis away from looks alone. Think about other reasons to value yourself: personality, brains, enthusiasm, friendliness, talents, kindness. Try making a list of all your good qualities, and ask trusted friends for their positive input too. It is often easier to think negative thoughts about yourself, but try hard to come up with positive ones. It can take some practice, but it's worth making the effort!

Celebrate your achievements, and take on new challenges a few steps at a time. Try learning some new skills, or taking up sport or other interests. You can also boost your self-confidence by trying assertiveness training, or learning acting, for example. If your self-esteem is very low, counselling or therapy can be a great help too.

Taking action

You can make a big change for yourself and those around you by rejecting prejudice. Don't make rude remarks about yourself or others because of the way you or they look. Avoid negative comments such as 'fat pig', 'thunder thighs', 'greedy slob', or spiteful remarks about skin colour, age, or body shape. Even if it's only meant as a joke, or is an 'affectionate' remark, it can still hurt feelings badly. Don't tease your friends for being short, having big ears or looking different, and stand by them if other people are bullying them about their looks. Stand up for yourself too, and report bullies to schoolteachers. Spend less time with people who put

'All the time I used to spend stressing about how I looked, I now spend playing music, seeing my friends, learning new things and travelling. I'm enjoying life to the full again.'
(Darren, aged 19)

you down by making unhelpful or harsh comments about your appearance.

If a magazine you read uses unhealthily thin models, why not write to the magazine editor to ask them to use models of different shapes and sizes? Or you could only buy magazines that show a range of body types and are more realistic. If you think a magazine is setting a good example, write to tell them you like what they are trying to do.

On a similar note, if you think a company is using models with eating disorders in their advertisements, or deliberately trying to make ordinary people feel bad about themselves, you can make a written complaint about the ad. If enough people write in, unhealthy ads can be changed or stopped. If that doesn't work, you can also boycott the company – don't buy their products. Some advertisements for diet and exercise products are dishonest and misleading. If you spot one, report it to the organization in your country that's responsible for advertising standards.

Arm yourself with knowledge. Learn more about body image, and explore and modify your beliefs about how bodies 'should' look. There are several organizations and books listed on page 62, if you would like to find out more.

Value the difference

Everyone is different and has a different variety of good qualities. You can help each other by showing appreciation of all the good points.

Glossary

abscess — a collection of pus caused by inflammation or bacteria.

abuse — using drugs for non-medical reasons. Sometimes called 'misuse' or 'recreational use'.

acne — common skin problem, especially in teenagers. Blackheads, whiteheads and spots appear on the face, chest, or back, under the influence of sex hormones.

anabolic steroids — synthetic drugs that have a similar action to the male sex hormone testosterone. Sometimes abused by body builders and athletes.

anorexia nervosa — eating disorder where food intake is restricted and a large amount of body weight is lost. Most common in young teenage girls.

anti-depressants — group of drugs that change the levels of various chemicals in the brain, relieving the symptoms of depression.

binge eating — eating a large amount of food and feeling unable to control the amount that is consumed. May be followed by feelings of anxiety and shame.

body dysmorphic disorder — disorder where a person wrongly believes that they are ugly, or that some part of their appearance is defective, such as their hair, nose or skin.

body image — the complex mental picture that someone has of their own body. It includes sensations, thoughts, and feelings.

bulimia nervosa — eating disorder where there are regular food binges and episodes of purging. Most common in older teenage girls, and women in their early twenties.

calorie — measurement of the energy that food provides. Sometimes energy is measured in joules instead.

CBT — cognitive behavioural therapy, a 'talking treatment' that helps people challenge unhelpful thought patterns or beliefs.

chronic dieting — reducing calorie intake for a period of months or years.

cosmetic — any process or product that is used to gain a particular appearance.

crash diet — an unhealthy form of dieting where someone severely restricts their food intake. Can cause mood swings and an urge to binge eat.

eczema — skin problem sometimes caused by allergies or contact with irritants.

emollient — substance with soothing or moisturizing effects on the skin.

gangrene — dead or decaying tissue caused by loss of blood supply or infection.

genetic — anything relating to genes. Genetic material is inherited from both parents, and is found in most cells in the human body in the form of chromosomes. It influences many characteristics such as height and eye colour.

hepatitis viruses — infections carried in the blood that may cause inflammation of the liver and other health problems.

HIV	Human Immunodeficiency Virus, the infection that causes AIDS.
hormone	a chemical substance that is released into the bloodstream and carried to certain cells where it attaches and causes changes in their metabolism.
laxatives	drugs and herbs that stimulate the bowels (guts) to work faster.
metabolism	all of the chemical processes taking place inside a living organism.
muscle dysmorphia	also called 'reverse anorexia'. A disorder where someone thinks their body is less muscular than it really is.
obesity	when someone weighs more than the recommended amount for their height.
plastic surgery	surgery to reconstruct the shape of the body, or to change the way someone looks.
psoriasis	skin problem where cells are replaced too quickly, causing red and flaky areas called plaques.
psychological	beginning in the mind.
puberty	the development process the human body goes through that makes it capable of sexual reproduction.
purging	attempting to get rid of food in an extreme way, such as by taking drugs or vomiting.
radiotherapy	treatment using radiation to kill cancerous cells.
reverse anorexia	another name for muscle dysmorphia.
self-esteem	feeling good about yourself. Liking and valuing yourself.
stroke	illness caused by a leaking or blocked blood vessel inside the brain. There may be temporary or permanent paralysis, or loss of consciousness.
subjective	based on a judgement or mental picture, rather than a fact or a measurement.
tuberculosis	infectious disease caused by tubercle bacteria, often affecting the lungs.
X-chromosome	one of the pieces of genetic material that determine someone's sex. The other sex chromosome is called 'Y'. Two Xs make a female, and an X plus a Y make a male.

Resources

Organizations

National Eating Disorders Association (USA)
603 Stewart Street, Suite 803, Seattle WA 98101

Tel: (206) 382-3587
email service: info@NationalEatingDisorders.org
Website: www.nationaleatingdisorders.org

Eating Disorders Association (UK)
103 Prince of Wales Road, Norwich NR1 1DW

Adult Helpline: 0845 634 1414 (open 8:30 to 20:30 weekdays)
Youthline: 0845 634 7650 (open 16:00 to 18:30 weekdays)
Text-phone service: 01603 753322 (open 8:30 to 20:30 weekdays)
e-mail service: helpmail@edauk.com
Website: www.edauk.com

American Counseling Association
5999 Stevenson Ave, Alexandria VA 22304

Toll-Free tel: (800) 347-6647
Website: www.counseling.org

British Association for Counselling and Psychotherapy
BACP House, 35-37 Albert Street, Rugby CV21 2SG

Tel: 0870 443 5252
email: bacp@bacp.co.uk
Website: www.bacp.co.uk

American Society of Plastic Surgeons
Plastic Surgery Educational Foundation
444 E. Algonquin Road, Arlington Heights IL 60005

Website: www.plasticsurgery.org

Books

Anita Naik, *Wise Guides: Eating,* Hodder Children's Books, 2005
Advice for teenagers on dieting and eating disorders, healthy eating, exercising and self-esteem.

Rita Freedman, *Bodylove: Learning to Like Our Looks and Ourselves*, Gurze Books, 2002
A practical guidebook, mainly aimed at women. Has been used as part of therapy by many eating disorder clinics.

Kimberly Kirberger, *No Body's Perfect: Stories by Teens about Body Image, Self-Acceptance, and the Search for Identity*, Scholastic Paperbacks, 2003

Janet Treasure, *Anorexia nervosa: A Survival Guide for Families, Friends and Sufferers*, Psychology Press 1997

Index